Horses and Ponies

François Bissonnette

Animal Books for Children Collection

Horses and Ponies

Hello!

My name is Passion, and I am a horse.

I belong to the *Equidae* family, also known as the horse family.

Unlike other animals, like pandas and elephants, which only live in certain parts of the world, horses are found all over the globe. There are over 58 million horses in the world.

It's hard to know exactly how many horse and pony breeds there are, but it's more than 300.

Horse breeds are loosely divided into three categories: light horses, heavy horses and ponies.

Light horses, like me, are the most common types of horses seen today.

We are smaller than heavy horses, but larger than ponies. We are fast and have good endurance. Humans use us for riding and light work.

Some of us are used for ranch work, others for racing or competition.

Heavy horses are powerful and gentle animals. That's why they are called "gentle giants".

They are used for farm work, parades and pulling carts and heavy loads.

Ponies are calm, gentle and friendly. They are perfect for children who are learning to ride.

The Shetland pony is one of the most popular ponies.

Just like the car of your mom or dad, we horses, have four speeds. The first speed is walk, the second is trot, the third is canter, and the fourth is gallop. On average, horses can gallop at a speed of 25 to 30 miles per hour (40 to 48 kilometers per hour).

The world record for a horse galloping over a short, sprint distance is 55 miles per hour (88 kilometers per hour).

We are herbivores, in other words, we eat plants. We mostly eat hay and grasses and drink a lot of water.

But we also like grains such as corn or oats, fruit such as apples, and vegetables such as carrots. But humans must slice the apples and carrots before feeding us so we don't choke.

Do you know that ponies and horses can sleep both lying down and standing up?

We can lock the muscles in our legs to sleep while standing without falling. We don't sleep for long period of time like humans do. We only sleep between 2 to 3 hours a day in short periods of time (about 15 minutes).

We have the biggest eyes of all land mammals. Our eyes are on the side of our head, not in the front like yours. Therefore, we have a range of vision of more than 350°. We only have a blind spot in front of our face and directly behind us.

Our sense of smell is not as good as that of a dog, but a lot better than that of humans.

A horse's hearing is also really good, and we can rotate our ears up to 180°.

A new baby horse, called a foal, can stand on its own feet and can walk and run around shortly following birth.

Did you know that the hoof wall is made of keratin just like your fingernail? A horse's hoof is always growing. A domesticated horse wears his hooves down faster than the wild horse. This is why humans put horseshoes on our hooves. They have to trim the hooves and replace the shoes every 4 to 6 weeks.

We can live 25 to 30 years. But there was a horse named Billy, born in England in 1760, who lived 62 years. There was also Sugar Puff a Shetland-Exmoor cross pony who dies at 56 years old.

A horse or pony is measured from the ground to the top of the withers, where the neck meets the back.

A light horse, usually range in height from 56 to 68 inches (142 to 173 cm). Heavy horse, are usually 64 inches to 72 inches (163 cm to 183 cm) high. Ponies are less than 58 inches (147 cm) high.

The biggest and tallest horse was a shire horse named Sampson. He was 86 inches (218 cm) high and his weight was estimated at 3,300 lbs (1,500 kilograms). Because of his size, he was renamed Mammoth.

The smallest horse was born in 1973, his name was Little Pumpkin. He was 14 inches (35.5 cm) tall and weighs only 20 pounds (9 kilograms).

Now, let's talk about our coat colors.

Horses and ponies come in a wide range of colors.

Bay coat horses have brown bodies with black manes, tails and black lower limbs. They also have black points on their faces and ears.

Chestnut horses have reddish brown coats. Manes and tails are usually the same color, but may be lighter.

Black horses have a pure black coat, with no brown hairs, but they may have white markings on the face or legs. Manes and tails are also black.

Gray horses are horses that have white or gray hairs, but even when they have only white hairs, they are not considered white, because they have black skin.

Brown horses have a mixture of brown and black hair and the manes and tails are dark brown. They are sometimes difficult to distinguish from black horses.

Cream or Cremello horses range from almost white to pale cream, and they have blue eyes.

Dun horses range in color from beige to brown with black or dark brown mane, tail, legs and tips of the ears. They also have a dorsal stripe.

Palomino horses have gold coat. Their manes and tails are lighter.

Pinto horses have a white coat with another color like brown, black or gold. They have large patches like cows.

Piebald is the name used for Pinto horses with patches of black and white.

Skewbald is used for Pinto horses with patches of white and any color except black.

Appaloosa horses have spots and splashes on their coat. They normally have stripes in their hooves.

Many horses and ponies have facial markings. Markings are areas of white hair on the face and legs.

Star marking is a small white mark on the forehead of the horse.

Stripe marking is a small white line stretching down the middle of the face.

Blaze marking is a large white line stretching down the middle of the face.

White face marking is similar to a blaze marking, but covering a larger area.

White, Stripe and Blaze markings

Horses nuzzle each other to establish their relationships.

Horses roll on the grass for pleasure and to clean their coat.

It's really fun to be a Horse! I spend my days, eating, walking and running around with my owner and being cuddled on by humans.

What a wonderful life!

Horses

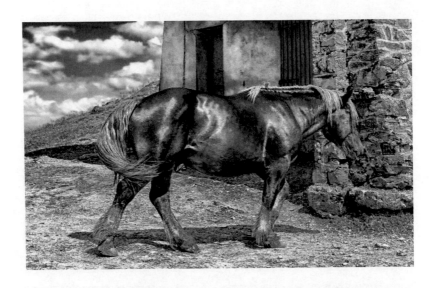

Ponies

Horses and Ponies

From the same collection

Free Bonus!
Your access to the VideoBook!

magicalchildrenbooks.com/en/horses-and-ponies/

Password: hopo542

Please don't share this link and this password with anyone. The author and the Videomaker have families to feed and the price of this Book is affordable. Thank you!

31079733R10039

Made in the USA
Middletown, DE
17 April 2016